WELCOME TO THE U.S.A.
NEW MEXICO

Written by Ann Heinrichs   Illustrated by Matt Kania
Content Adviser: Dr. John Kessell, Historian, University
of New Mexico, Albuquerque, New Mexico

The Child's World

Published in the United States of America by The Child's World®
PO Box 326 • Chanhassen, MN 55317-0326
800-599-READ • www.childsworld.com

Photo Credits
Cover: New Mexico Department of Tourism; frontispiece: New Mexico
Department of Tourism.

Interior: Bradbury Science Museum: 25; Brand X Pictures: 10; Corbis: 13
(George H. H. Huey), 16 (Bettmann); Intel Computers: 26; Catherine Karnow/
Corbis: 9, 33; Library of Congress: 20; New Mexico Department of Tourism:
6, 14 (Gary Romero), 21, 29 (Mark Stauffer), 30 (Dan Monaghan), 34
(Mark Nohl); New Mexico Institute of Mining and Tech: 22; El Rancho de las
Golondrinas: 17; Preciliana Sandoval: 18.

Acknowledgments
The Child's World®: Mary Berendes, Publishing Director

Editorial Directions, Inc.: E. Russell Primm, Editorial Director; Katie Marsico, Associate
Editor; Judith Shiffer, Assistant Editor; Matt Messbarger, Editorial Assistant; Susan
Hindman, Copy Editor; Melissa McDaniel, Proofreader; Kevin Cunningham, Peter
Garnham, Matt Messbarger, Olivia Nellums, Chris Simms, Molly Symmonds, Katherine
Trickle, Carl Stephen Wender, Fact Checkers; Tim Griffin/IndexServ, Indexer; Cian
Loughlin O'Day, Photo Researcher and Editor

The Design Lab: Kathleen Petelinsek, Design and art production

Library of Congress Cataloging-in-Publication Data
Heinrichs, Ann.
  New Mexico / by Ann Heinrichs.
    p. cm. – (Welcome to the U.S.A.)
  Includes index.
  ISBN 1-59296-379-X (library bound : alk. paper) 1. New Mexico—Juvenile literature.
I. Title.
  F796.3.H453 2006
  978.9–dc22   2005000531

Ann Heinrichs is the author
of more than 100 books
for children and young
adults. She has also enjoyed
successful careers as a
children's book editor and
an advertising copywriter.
Ann grew up in Fort Smith,
Arkansas, and lives in
Chicago, Illinois.

About the Author
Ann Heinrichs

Matt Kania loves maps and, as
a kid, dreamed of making them.
In school he studied geography
and cartography, and today he
makes maps for a living. Matt's
favorite thing about drawing
maps is learning about the places
they represent. Many of the maps
he has created can be found in
books, magazines, videos, Web
sites, and public places.

About the
Map Illustrator
Matt Kania

On the cover: This scenic mesa is part of the Zuni Pueblo.
On page one: Ride the Cumbres & Toltec train through the San Juan Mountains.

OUR NEW MEXICO TRIP

New Mexico's Nickname:
The Land of Enchantment

How about a trip through New Mexico? You're sure to have a great time!

You'll meet Geronimo and Billy the Kid. You'll explore forests, deserts, and caves. You'll see kangaroo rats and wild pigs. You'll even learn about visitors from outer space!

Are you curious? Then hop aboard and buckle your seat belt. We're off on a big adventure!

WELCOME TO NEW MEXICO

As you travel through New Mexico, watch for all the interesting facts along the way.

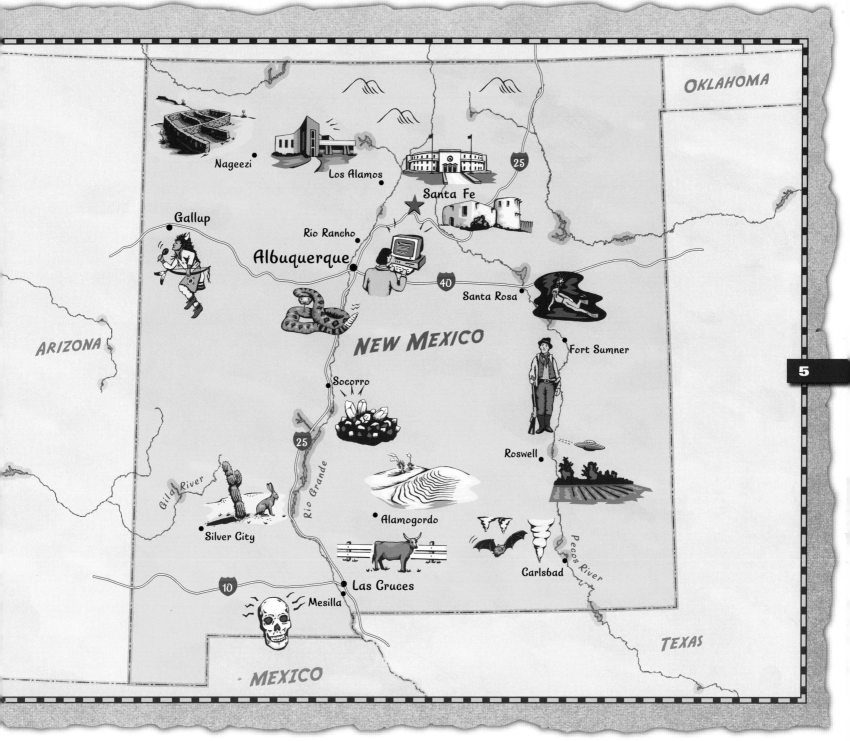

OKLAHOMA

Nageezi

Los Alamos

Santa Fe

25

Gallup

Rio Rancho

Albuquerque

40

Santa Rosa

NEW MEXICO

Fort Sumner

ARIZONA

Socorro

25

Gila River

Rio Grande

Silver City

Alamogordo

Roswell

Carlsbad

Pecos River

Las Cruces

10

Mesilla

MEXICO

TEXAS

Want to go underground? Explore the natural wonders of Carlsbad Caverns.

About 300,000 bats fly out of Carlsbad Caverns every evening!

Put on your knee pads. You might find yourself crawling through cave tunnels! You're entering Carlsbad Caverns. But you don't *have to* crawl. You can stroll along if you'd like.

New Mexico has many different land features. The Rocky Mountains reach into northern New Mexico. They include the Sangre de Cristo Mountains. That's the state's biggest mountain range. The northwest is rough and rugged. It has many canyons and rocky cliffs. Level plains cover eastern New Mexico. Thousands of cattle and sheep graze there. Deserts cover much of the state. Some are rocky, while others are sandy. White Sands National Monument is in the south near Alamogordo. Its sand is—you guessed it—white!

Carlsbad Caverns is among the world's largest cave systems.

Rocky Mountains

Gavilan •

Wheeler Peak

Sangre de Cristo Mountains

OKLAHOMA

Highest Temperature: near Carlsbad June 27, 1994 122°F (50°C)

Lowest Temperature: Gavilan February 1, 1951 −50°F (−46°C)

ARIZONA

Yikes . . . some of these caves have spooky names! Like Hall of the White Giant and Spider Cave.

Rio Grande River

TEXAS

Alamogordo •

White Sands National Monument

Carlsbad •

Eddy County

HIGHEST AND LOWEST POINTS
Highest: Wheeler Peak at 13,161 feet (4,011 m)
Lowest: Red Bluff Reservoir in Eddy County at 2,817 feet (859 m)

The Rio Grande is New Mexico's major river. It runs through the state from north to south.

MEXICO

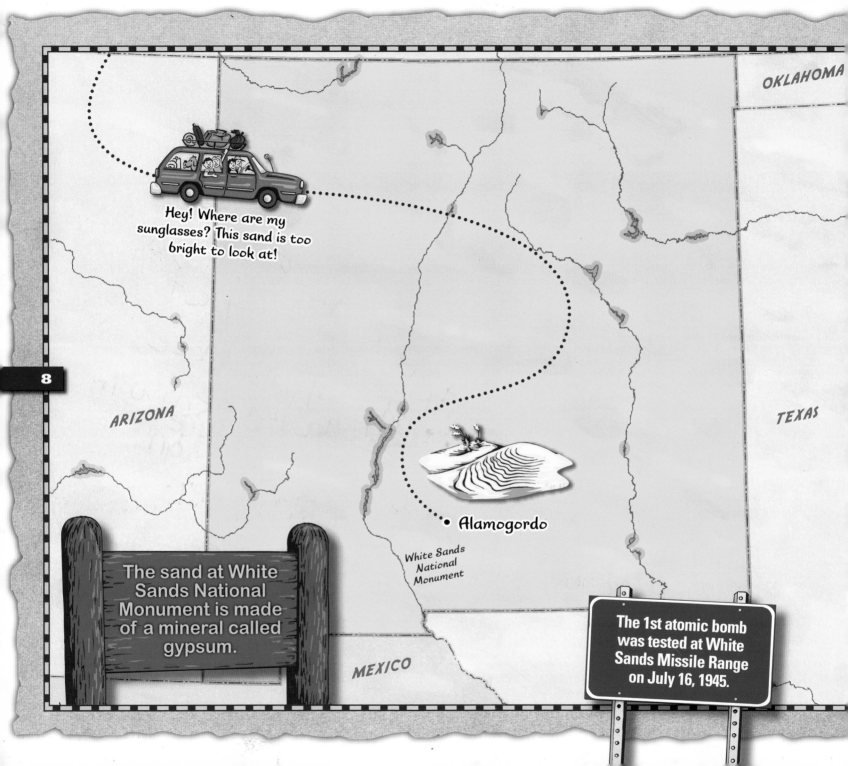

The New Mexico Museum of Space History is in Alamogordo.

White Sands National Monument is an awesome sight. Its sand almost looks like glistening snow! It stretches as far as the eye can see. Some sand is heaped up in big dunes. In other places, it's in wavy ripples.

Few animals live here. Some have developed ways to blend in. One type of mouse and one type of lizard are almost completely white! This coloring protects them in the sand.

People can't visit some parts of the White Sands area. The U.S. government tests missiles there. The first **atomic bomb** was tested there, too.

A beach with no water nearby? A boy buries himself in a dune at White Sands National Monument.

9

10

Roadrunners can fly, but they mostly walk or run on the ground.

Hike through the thick forests of Gila Wilderness. It's like hiking through an outdoor zoo!

You might see mountain lions, coyotes, and bears. Be still and don't bother them, though. They could be dangerous.

You'll also see deer, antelope, and wild turkeys. You might even see a javelina, or peccary. It's a kind of wild pig.

New Mexico is home to many other animals. Bighorn sheep live in the high mountains. Kangaroo rats live in dry desert regions. They hop really far with their long hind legs.

And don't forget the state bird. It's the roadrunner. Beep-beep!

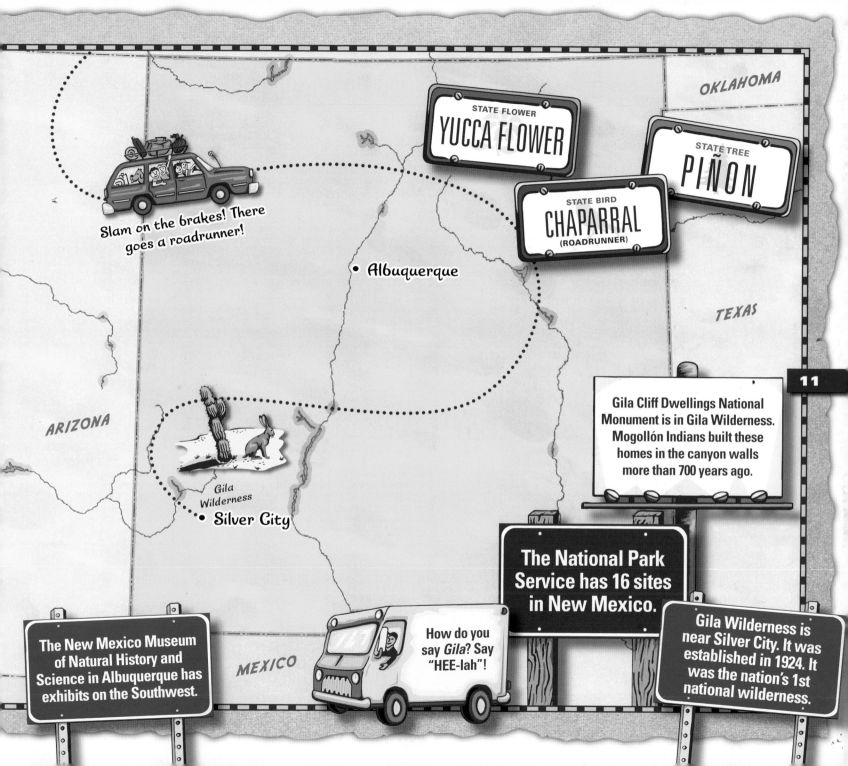

STATE FLOWER
YUCCA FLOWER

STATE TREE
PIÑON

STATE BIRD
CHAPARRAL
(ROADRUNNER)

OKLAHOMA

TEXAS

ARIZONA

MEXICO

Slam on the brakes! There goes a roadrunner!

• Albuquerque

Gila Wilderness

• Silver City

Gila Cliff Dwellings National Monument is in Gila Wilderness. Mogollón Indians built these homes in the canyon walls more than 700 years ago.

The National Park Service has 16 sites in New Mexico.

The New Mexico Museum of Natural History and Science in Albuquerque has exhibits on the Southwest.

How do you say *Gila*? Say "HEE-lah"!

Gila Wilderness is near Silver City. It was established in 1924. It was the nation's 1st national wilderness.

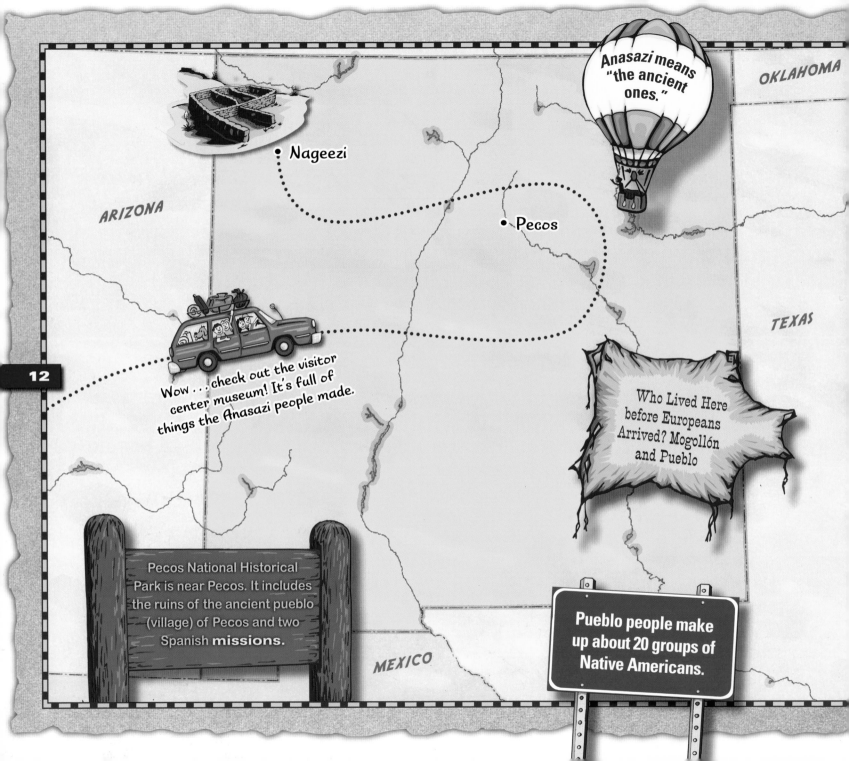

Chaco Culture National Historical Park

The Pueblo Bonito ruins at Chaco Canyon have more than 600 rooms!

Think about the building where you live. How many rooms does it have? Now imagine a building with more than 600 rooms. That's what **Pueblo** Bonito is like. It's a building in Chaco **Culture** National Historical Park near Nageezi. People called the Anasazi built it.

The Anasazi lived here more than 1,000 years ago. They built an amazing city. It had buildings, roads, dams, and earthen mounds. The Anasazi farmed and hunted. They traded with other peoples for goods they needed.

The Anasazi's **descendants** are still alive today. They are called the Pueblo people. They live in New Mexico and Arizona.

The people who lived at the Chaco site are often called the Chaco Anasazi.

Let's dance! Native Americans wear colorful costumes at the Inter-Tribal Ceremonial.

Gallup's Inter-Tribal Indian Ceremonial

The Inter-Tribal Indian Ceremonial is a dazzling festival. Dozens of Native American groups take part. You'll see them perform **traditional** dances. Their costumes are a swirl of colors! There's a rodeo, complete with bull-riding. And you can eat delicious Indian foods.

It's said that New Mexico has three cultures. They are Native American, Hispanic, and Anglo. Anglos are white people descended from Europeans.

Some Indians live on **reservations.** Others live in pueblos. The major groups are Pueblo, Navajo, and Apache. New Mexico's Hispanics are mainly descended from Spaniards and Mexicans. Their native Spanish language is heard around the state.

POPULATION OF LARGEST CITIES

Albuquerque 448,607
Las Cruces 74,267
Santa Fe 62,203

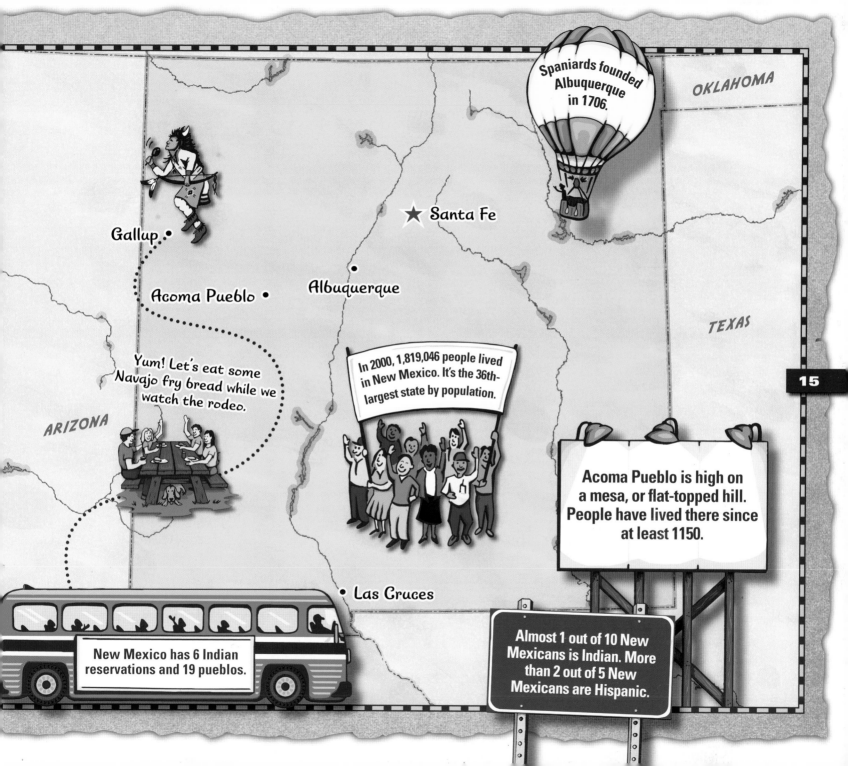

Spaniards founded Albuquerque in 1706.

OKLAHOMA

★ Santa Fe

Gallup •

Acoma Pueblo •

• Albuquerque

TEXAS

Yum! Let's eat some Navajo fry bread while we watch the rodeo.

ARIZONA

In 2000, 1,819,046 people lived in New Mexico. It's the 36th-largest state by population.

Acoma Pueblo is high on a mesa, or flat-topped hill. People have lived there since at least 1150.

• Las Cruces

New Mexico has 6 Indian reservations and 19 pueblos.

Almost 1 out of 10 New Mexicans is Indian. More than 2 out of 5 New Mexicans are Hispanic.

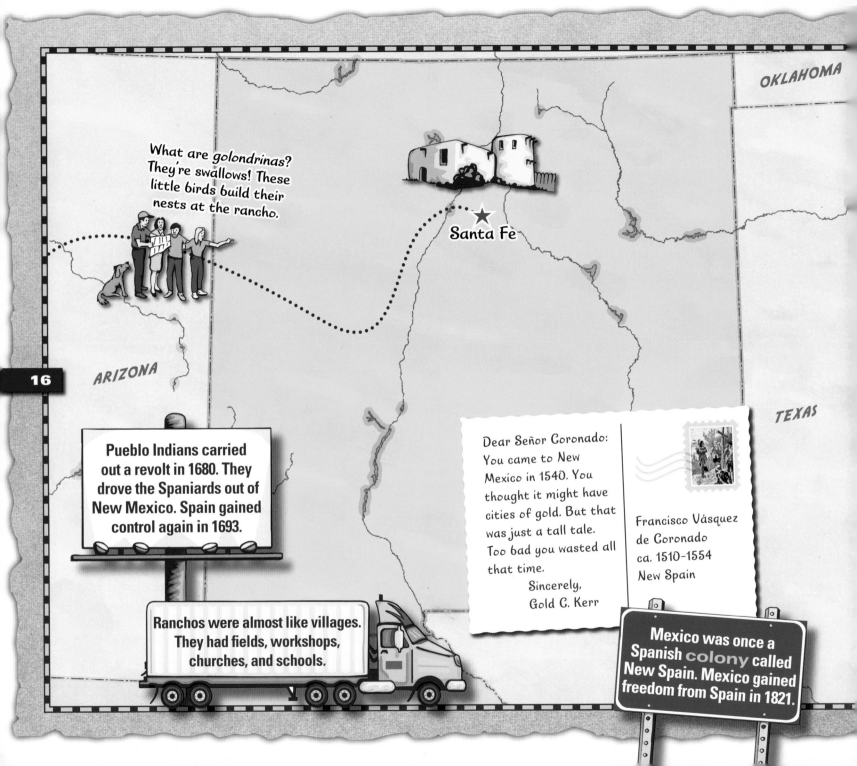

OKLAHOMA

What are golondrinas? They're swallows! These little birds build their nests at the rancho.

★ Santa Fe

ARIZONA

16

TEXAS

Pueblo Indians carried out a revolt in 1680. They drove the Spaniards out of New Mexico. Spain gained control again in 1693.

Dear Señor Coronado:
You came to New Mexico in 1540. You thought it might have cities of gold. But that was just a tall tale. Too bad you wasted all that time.
    Sincerely,
    Gold C. Kerr

Francisco Vásquez de Coronado
ca. 1510–1554
New Spain

Ranchos were almost like villages. They had fields, workshops, churches, and schools.

Mexico was once a Spanish colony called New Spain. Mexico gained freedom from Spain in 1821.

Santa Fe's El Rancho de las Golondrinas

A woman makes a long string of chili peppers. It's called a ristra. She will hang it up to dry. It's a welcome sign for visitors.

This woman works at El Rancho de las Golondrinas. It's a living history museum. People's clothes and activities show life in the 1700s. That's when this rancho, or farm, was built.

Spain ruled New Mexico for more than 200 years. During that time, many Spaniards had ranchos there. They and the Indians did the farmwork. Spanish priests opened missions, too. They taught Christianity to the Indians.

New Mexico came under Mexico's rule in 1821. Then Americans and Mexicans fought the Mexican War (1846–1848). The United States won and took over New Mexico.

Not your typical welcome mat! These women are making ristras that will be hung on doors.

It's a day for dancing! Residents of Mesilla celebrate Día de los Muertos.

Cities all over the state celebrate Día de los Muertos. Some of the biggest festivals are in Las Cruces and Mesilla.

Día de los Muertos in Mesilla

People are wearing skeleton masks. They're eating candy shaped like skulls. Is this some kind of Halloween festival? In a way, it is. It's *Día de los Muertos*. That's Spanish for "Day of the Dead."

Halloween began as a Christian holiday. It was the day before All Saints' Day—November 1. The next day is All Souls' Day. That day, November 2, people honor loved ones who have died. It's called Día de los Muertos in Hispanic culture.

Mesilla's celebration is very colorful. Altars to the dead fill the town square. They're decorated with candles, flowers, and photos. It's not a sad festival at all. It's a way to celebrate a loved one's life!

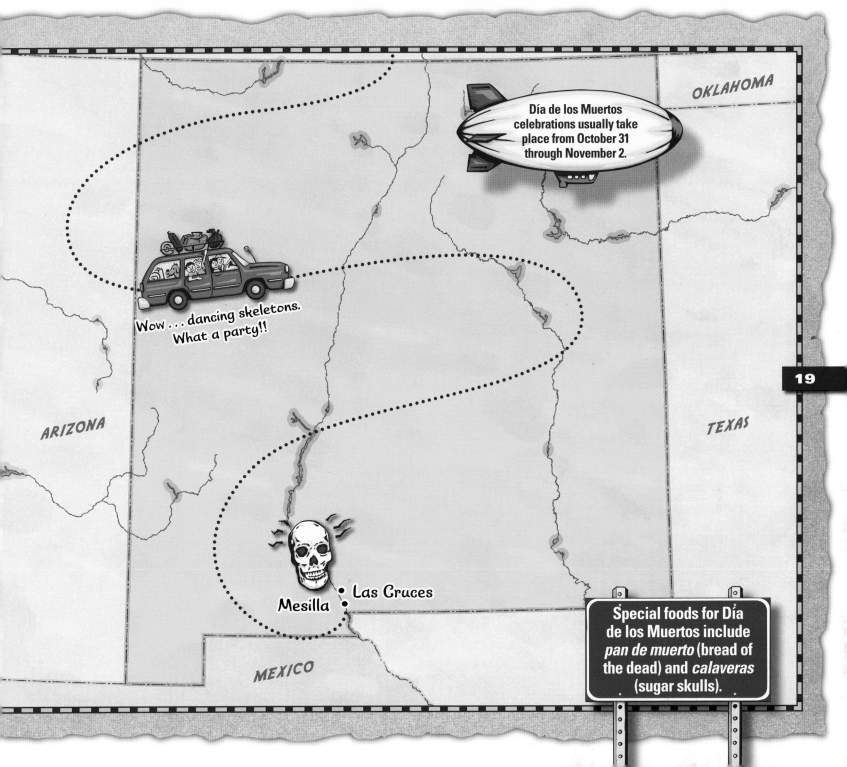

Día de los Muertos celebrations usually take place from October 31 through November 2.

Wow . . . dancing skeletons. What a party!!

OKLAHOMA

ARIZONA

TEXAS

19

Mesilla • Las Cruces

MEXICO

Special foods for Día de los Muertos include *pan de muerto* (bread of the dead) and *calaveras* (sugar skulls).

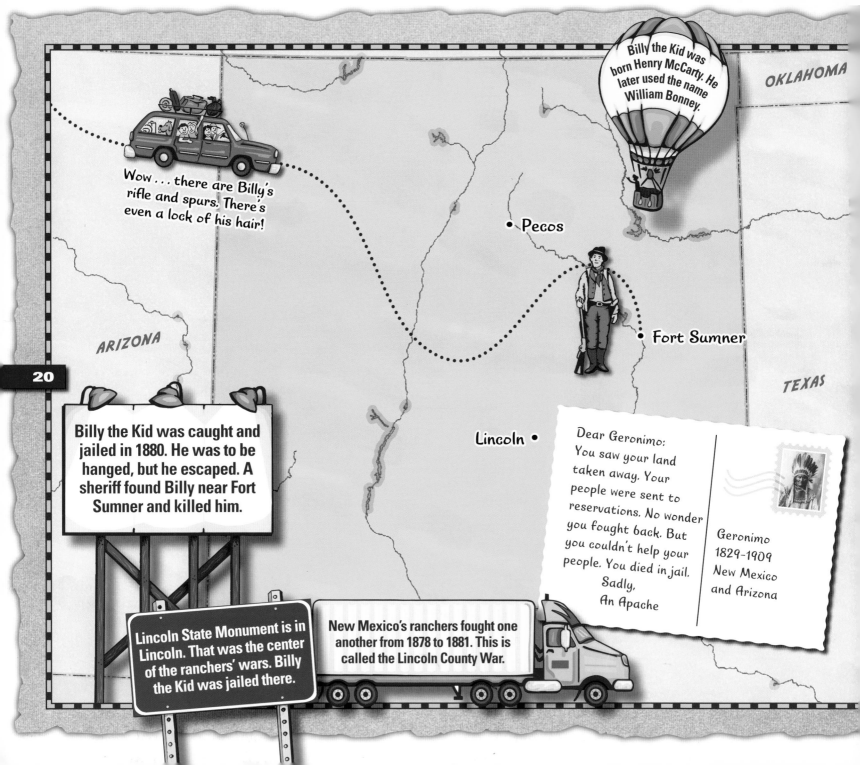

OKLAHOMA

Billy the Kid was born Henry McCarty. He later used the name William Bonney.

Wow . . . there are Billy's rifle and spurs. There's even a lock of his hair!

• Pecos

ARIZONA

• Fort Sumner

TEXAS

Billy the Kid was caught and jailed in 1880. He was to be hanged, but he escaped. A sheriff found Billy near Fort Sumner and killed him.

Lincoln •

Dear Geronimo:
You saw your land taken away. Your people were sent to reservations. No wonder you fought back. But you couldn't help your people. You died in jail.
Sadly,
An Apache

Geronimo
1829-1909
New Mexico
and Arizona

Lincoln State Monument is in Lincoln. That was the center of the ranchers' wars. Billy the Kid was jailed there.

New Mexico's ranchers fought one another from 1878 to 1881. This is called the Lincoln County War.

WANTED! Be sure to visit famous outlaw Billy the Kid's grave.

Reward—$5,000—Billy the Kid—Dead or Alive!

Billy the Kid was a famous outlaw. Just visit the Billy the Kid Museum. You'll learn all about his wild life. And you'll see posters for his capture.

Billy lived when New Mexico was a U.S. territory. He got involved in a war between ranchers. He ended up stealing cattle and killing people.

Meanwhile, Indians and settlers fought many battles. The Indians tried to hold on to their lands. In the end, they lost. Apache and Navajo people were forced onto reservations. Apache chief Geronimo kept fighting until 1886. Finally, he had to give up, too.

Glorieta National Battlefield is near Pecos. It's the site of an 1862 battle during the Civil War (1861–1865).

You'll see gold, silver, and precious jewels at the Mineral Museum.

New Mexico was the 47th state to enter the Union. It joined on January 6, 1912.

The Mineral Museum in Socorro

Look around the Mineral Museum. It's a real feast for your eyes. You see gold and silver. Precious gems are sparkling everywhere. It looks like someone emptied a treasure chest!

This museum's nickname is Coronado's Treasure Chest. Coronado explored New Mexico in about 1540. He was looking for gold. He didn't find any, though.

Coronado just didn't look hard enough. New Mexicans discovered gold in 1828. More gold was found in the 1860s. Then miners found silver, too.

Mining quickly became a big business in New Mexico. Thousands of people rushed in to get rich. Mining towns sprang up overnight. Many of them shut down just as quickly. They turned into **ghost towns.**

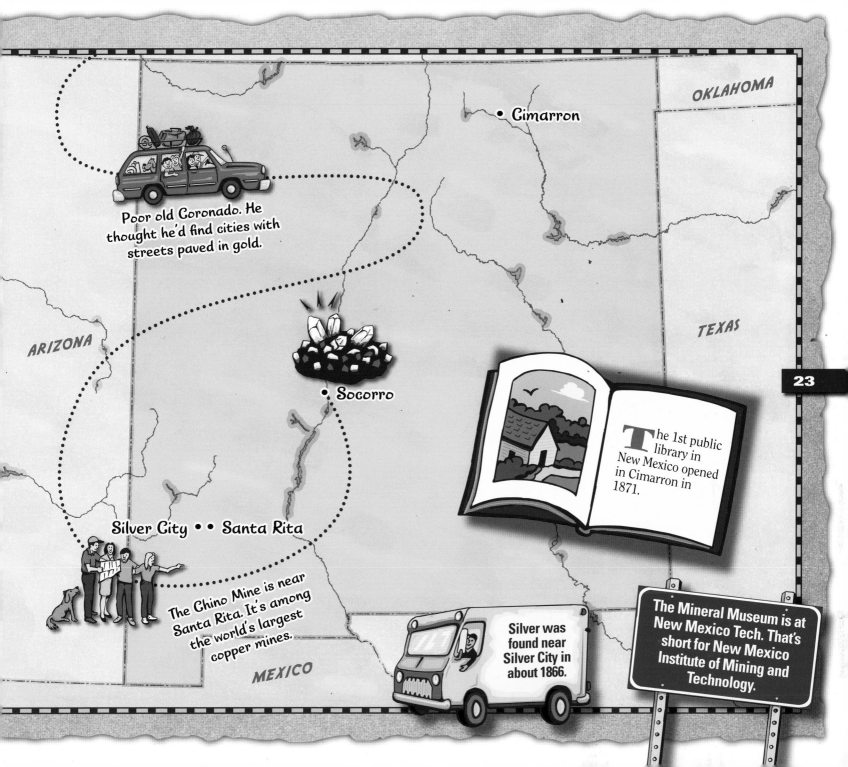

Poor old Coronado. He thought he'd find cities with streets paved in gold.

• Cimarron

OKLAHOMA

TEXAS

ARIZONA

• Socorro

The 1st public library in New Mexico opened in Cimarron in 1871.

Silver City •• Santa Rita

The Chino Mine is near Santa Rita. It's among the world's largest copper mines.

MEXICO

Silver was found near Silver City in about 1866.

The Mineral Museum is at New Mexico Tech. That's short for New Mexico Institute of Mining and Technology.

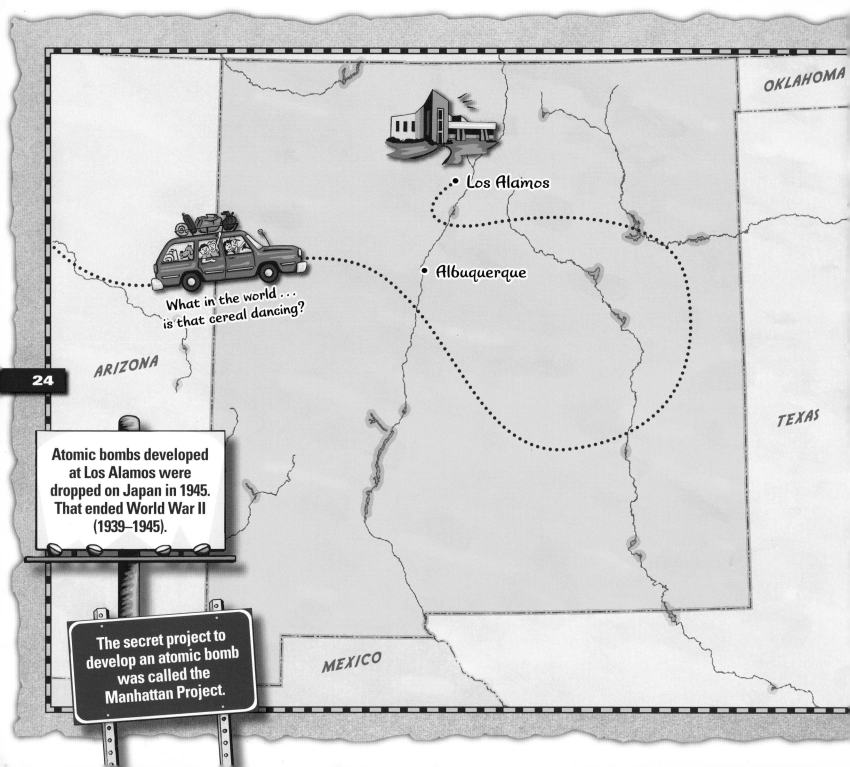

OKLAHOMA

• Los Alamos

What in the world . . .
is that cereal dancing?

• Albuquerque

ARIZONA

TEXAS

Atomic bombs developed
at Los Alamos were
dropped on Japan in 1945.
That ended World War II
(1939–1945).

The secret project to
develop an atomic bomb
was called the
Manhattan Project.

MEXICO

Get electric! A father and son explore the Bradbury Science Museum.

Do you like science? Then you'll love Bradbury Science Museum. There are lots of hands-on displays. And scientists there often put on shows. Maybe you can catch the electricity show. Electricity is used to make cereal dance!

Los Alamos National Laboratory operates this museum. Scientists worked at Los Alamos in the 1940s. They developed the first atomic bomb.

New Mexico's science activities kept growing. Sandia National Laboratories opened in Albuquerque. Scientists there work with **nuclear energy.**

Scientists at Los Alamos are still working, too. They're finding new ways to use nuclear energy.

Ever wonder how your computer works? Visit the Intel Visitors Center for a tour.

Intel Computers at Rio Rancho

Intel is a big computer company near Albuquerque in Rancho Rio. It makes computer chips. Those are tiny parts that make computers work.

Stop by the Intel Visitors Center. It's like a computer museum. The first thing you see is a bunny suit. That's what it's called, anyhow. Workers wear the suits in the factory. This keeps the computer chips super clean!

Computer equipment is New Mexico's major factory product. Some factories make telephone parts. Food, clothes, and many other goods are also made there.

Mining is a big business, too. New Mexico once mined lots of gold and silver. Today, it mines oil and natural gas. Miners are also digging out coal and copper.

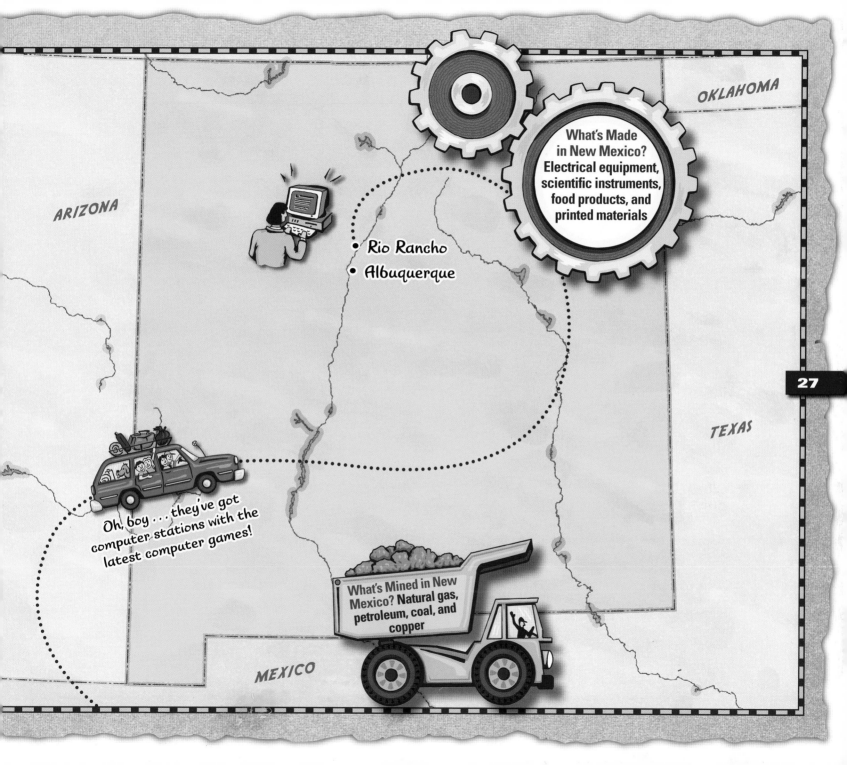

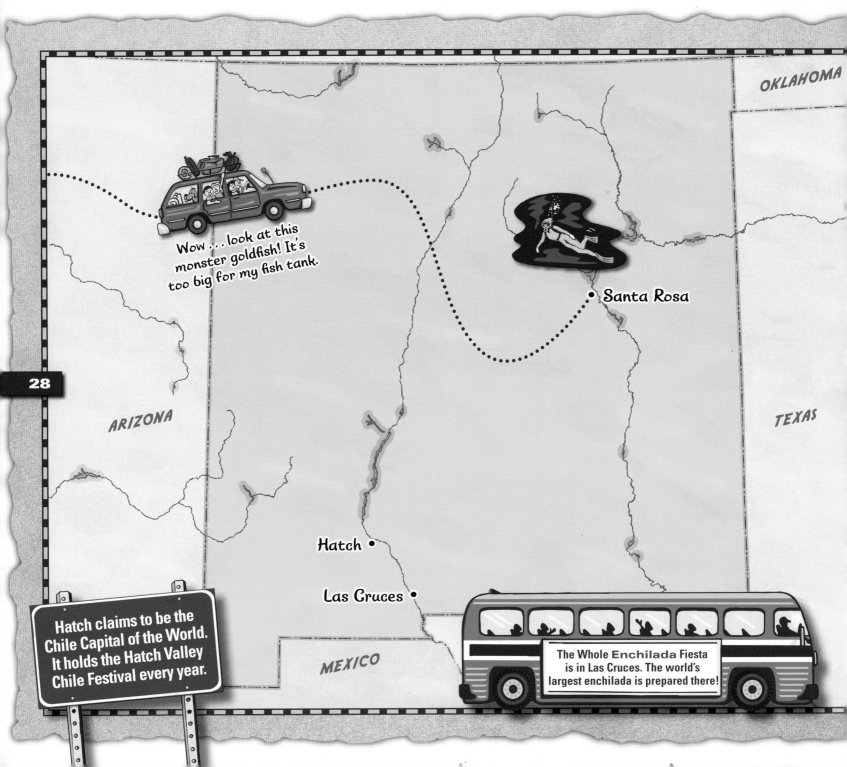

OKLAHOMA

Wow ... look at this monster goldfish! It's too big for my fish tank.

Santa Rosa

ARIZONA

TEXAS

Hatch •

Las Cruces •

Hatch claims to be the Chile Capital of the World. It holds the Hatch Valley Chile Festival every year.

MEXICO

The Whole Enchilada Fiesta is in Las Cruces. The world's largest enchilada is prepared there!

Swimming in Santa Rosa's Blue Hole

Dive into the clear blue water. You see goldfish swimming around you! You're in a deep pool called the Blue Hole. It's a favorite spot for divers.

New Mexico has lots of places to have fun. Swimmers and boaters love Santa Rosa's fifteen lakes. The Blue Hole is just one of them.

Some people enjoy New Mexico's deserts. They see cactuses and lots of desert animals. Others like to climb rocks and mountains. In the winter, snow falls in the mountains. Then people ski down the snowy slopes.

Many towns have rodeos. Real cowboys come to show off their skills. And there are festivals all year long. They celebrate New Mexico's many cultures.

Rope him in, cowboy! Rodeos are a popular New Mexico attraction.

Many laws are passed at the capitol in Santa Fe.

New Mexico's state capitol is called the Roundhouse. Just visit it, and you'll see why. It's round! It's built in the shape of the Zia.

The Zia is a very old Pueblo Indian symbol. It stands for the Sun. Rays shine from the top, bottom, and sides. They stand for the four directions and four seasons.

Inside the capitol are the state government offices. New Mexico has three branches of government. One branch makes the state's laws. The governor leads another branch. It carries out the laws. Judges make up the third branch. They decide whether someone has broken the law.

Welcome to Santa Fe, the capital of New Mexico!

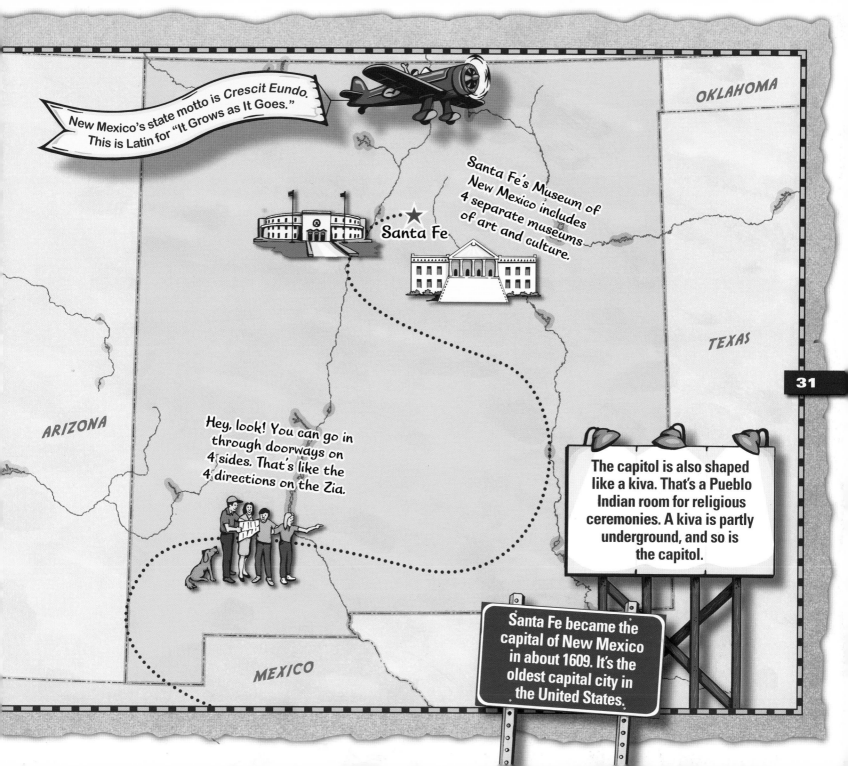

New Mexico's state motto is Crescit Eundo. This is Latin for "It Grows as It Goes."

Santa Fe's Museum of New Mexico includes 4 separate museums of art and culture.

Santa Fe

OKLAHOMA

TEXAS

ARIZONA

Hey, look! You can go in through doorways on 4 sides. That's like the 4 directions on the Zia.

The capitol is also shaped like a kiva. That's a Pueblo Indian room for religious ceremonies. A kiva is partly underground, and so is the capitol.

Santa Fe became the capital of New Mexico in about 1609. It's the oldest capital city in the United States.

MEXICO

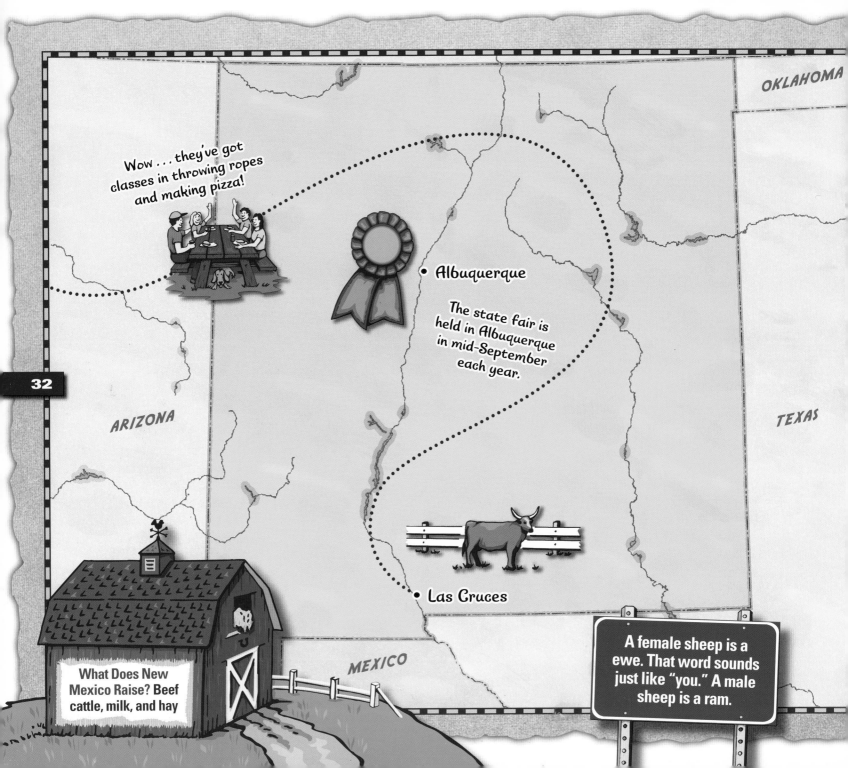

The Farm and Ranch Heritage Museum in Las Cruces

Watch a farmer milk a cow. Then try it yourself on a model cow. Watch a blacksmith make iron tools. Then eat some freshly baked **tortillas.**

You're visiting the Farm and Ranch Heritage Museum in Las Cruces. It shows how New Mexicans farmed for 3,000 years.

Farming has always been important to New Mexico. Early peoples grew corn, beans, and squash. Today, cattle ranching is the top farm activity. Thousands of cattle graze across the eastern plains. Many ranchers raise sheep, too.

Hay, chili peppers, and onions are leading crops. Crops grow best in the river valleys. Water is brought to the fields through **irrigation.**

That's one spicy pepper! Green chili peppers are harvested on this New Mexico farm.

The International UFO Museum in Roswell

Do you believe there is life on other planets? Visit the UFO Museum and find out!

The UFO Museum has an online newsletter for kids. It's at http://iufomrc.org/kids.shtml.

Do you believe in UFOs? Those are unidentified flying objects. If you do, you've got to visit Roswell. Head straight for the International UFO Museum!

Many people believe a UFO crashed in Roswell. They believe it was a spaceship. They think aliens were aboard. What became of these creatures from another planet? That's what everyone is wondering.

Believe the story or not. It's for you to decide! In any case, you'll enjoy the museum. You'll learn about UFO sightings around the world. You'll see exhibits about the Roswell crash. And you'll learn about lots of other weird happenings. How can you resist?

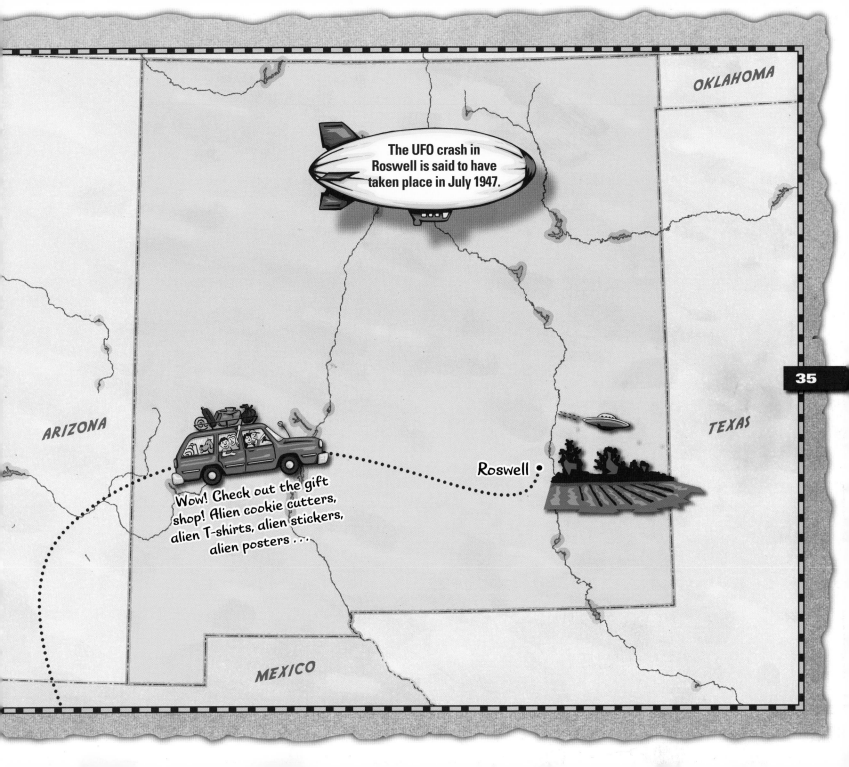

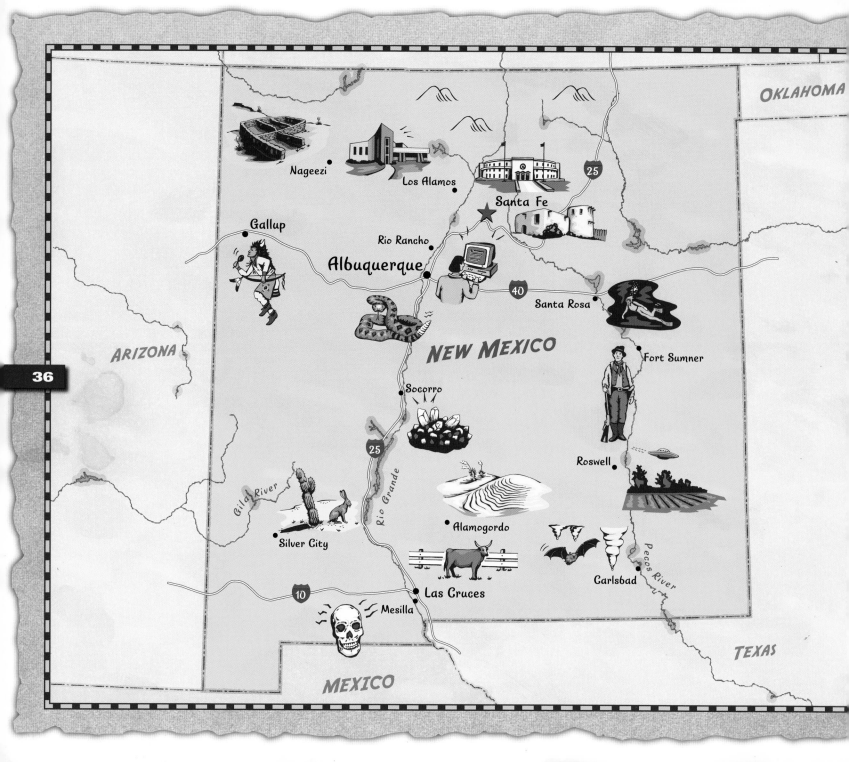

OKLAHOMA

Nageezi

Los Alamos

Santa Fe

25

Gallup

Rio Rancho

Albuquerque

40

Santa Rosa

NEW MEXICO

Fort Sumner

ARIZONA

Socorro

Roswell

Gila River

25

Rio Grande

Silver City

Alamogordo

Carlsbad

Pecos River

10

Las Cruces

Mesilla

TEXAS

MEXICO

OUR TRIP

We visited many amazing places on our trip! We also met a lot of interesting people along the way. Look at the map on the left. Use your finger to trace all the places we have been.

How many bats fly out of Carlsbad Caverns every evening? See page 6 for the answer.

How fast can roadrunners run? Page 10 has the answer.

How long have people lived in Acoma Pueblo? See page 15 for the answer.

What are golondrinas? Look on page 16 for the answer.

What was Billy the Kid's name when he was born? Page 20 has the answer.

What was the Manhattan Project? Turn to page 24 for the answer.

Where are the world's largest enchiladas prepared? Look on page 28 and find out!

What's the oldest capital city in the United States? Turn to page 31 for the answer.

That was a great trip! We have traveled all over New Mexico!
There are a few places we didn't have time for, though. Next time, we plan to visit the American International Rattlesnake Museum in Albuquerque. The museum is home to snakes from North, Central, and South America. It contains the world's largest live collection of different types of rattlesnakes.

More Places to Visit in New Mexico

WORDS TO KNOW

atomic bomb (uh-TOM-ik BOM) a powerful bomb made by splitting tiny particles called atoms

colony (KOL-uh-nee) a land with ties to another country

culture (KUHL-chur) a people's customs, beliefs, and ways of life

descendants (di-SEND-uhnts) children, grandchildren, great-grandchildren, and so on

enchilada (en-chi-LAH-dah) a tortilla wrapped around a filling with chili sauce on top

ghost towns (GOHST TOUNS) towns where everyone has moved out

irrigation (ihr-ruh-GAY-shuhn) a way of bringing water to fields through pipes or ditches

missions (MISH-uhnz) centers where religious people try to spread their faith

nuclear energy (NOO-clee-ur EN-ur-jee) the energy released when atoms are split

pueblo (PWEB-loh) a village or a Native American building with many homes inside

reservations (rez-ur-VAY-shuhnz) lands where Native American groups have been moved

tortillas (tor-TEE-yuhz) round, flat bread made with corn or flour

traditional (truh-DISH-uh-nul) following long-held customs

New Mexico covers 121,356 square miles (314,309 sq km). It's the 5th-largest state in size.

STATE SYMBOLS

State animal: Black bear

State bird: Chaparral (roadrunner)

State cookie: Bizcochito

State fish: Native New Mexico cutthroat trout

State flower: Yucca flower

State fossil: *Coelophysis*

State gem: Turquoise

State grass: Blue grama

State insect: Tarantula hawk wasp

State tree: Piñon

State vegetables: Chile and frijole

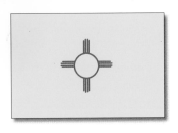

State flag

State seal

STATE SONG

"O, Fair New Mexico"

Words and music by Elizabeth Garrett, daughter of Pat Garrett,
the legendary sheriff who killed Billy the Kid

Under a sky of azure, where balmy breezes blow;
Kissed by the golden sunshine, is Nuevo Mejico.
Home of the Montezuma, with fiery heart aglow,
State of the deeds historic, is Nuevo Mejico.

Chorus:
O, fair New Mexico, we love, we love you so,
Our hearts with pride o'erflow,
No matter where we go.
O, fair New Mexico, we love, we love you so,
The grandest state to know—New Mexico.

Rugged and high sierras, with deep canyons below;
Dotted with fertile valleys, is Nuevo Mejico.
Fields full of sweet alfalfa, richest perfumes bestow,
State of apple blossoms, is Nuevo Mejico.

Days that are full of heart-dreams, nights when the
    Moon hangs low;
Beaming its benediction o'er Nuevo Mejico.
Land with its bright mañana, coming through weal and woe;
State of our esperanza, is Nuevo Mejico.

FAMOUS PEOPLE

Adams, Ansel (1902–1984), photographer

Anaya, Rudolfo (1937–), children's author

Blume, Judy (1938–), children's author

Bunche, Ralph (1904–1971), Nobel Peace Prize recipient

Carson, Christopher "Kit" (1809–1868), hunter and guide

Chavez, Dennis (1888–1962), politician and humanitarian

El Popé, (ca. 1630–ca. 1692), Pueblo hero

Geronimo (1829–1909), Apache Indian leader

Goddard, Robert (1882–1945), rocket scientist

Gutierrez, Sid (1951–), astronaut

Hanna, William (1910–2001), cartoonist

Hillerman, Tony (1925–), author

Hilton, Conrad N. (1887–1979), hotel executive

James, Rebecca Salsbury (1891–1968), artist

Lamy, Jean-Baptiste (1814–1888), Catholic bishop and humanitarian

Lopez, Nancy (1957–), professional golfer

Martinez, Maria (ca. 1886–1980), potter

McCarty, Henry "Billy the Kid" (1859–1881), famous outlaw

Moore, Demi (1962–), actor

O'Keeffe, Georgia (1887–1986), artist

Unser, Bobby (1934–), Al Sr. (1939–), Al Jr. (1962–), auto racers

Victorio (ca. 1825–1880), Apache chief

TO FIND OUT MORE

At the Library

Hayes, Joe, and Joseph Daniel Fiedler (illustrator). *Juan Verdades: The Man Who Could Not Tell a Lie.* New York: Orchard Books, 2001.

McDermott, Gerald. *Arrow to the Sun: A Pueblo Indian Tale.* New York: Viking Press, 1974.

Rasmussen, R. Kent, and Kimberly L. Dawson Kurnizki (illustrator). *Pueblo.* Vero Beach, Fla.: Rourke Book Co., 2001.

Welch, Catherine A. *Geronimo.* Minneapolis: Lerner Publications Co., 2004.

Winter, Jeanette. *My Name Is Georgia: A Portrait.* San Diego: Silver Whistle/Harcourt Brace, 1998.

On the Web

Visit our home page for lots of links about New Mexico: *http://www.childsworld.com/links*

Note to Parents, Teachers, and Librarians: We routinely verify our Web links to make sure they are safe, active sites—so encourage your readers to check them out!

Places to Visit or Contact

Historical Society of New Mexico
PO Box 1912
Santa Fe, NM 87504
For more information about the history of New Mexico

New Mexico Department of Tourism
491 Old Santa Fe Trail
Lamy Building
Santa Fe, NM 87501
800/733-6396
For more information about traveling in New Mexico

INDEX

Bye, Land of Enchantment.
We had a great time.
We'll come back soon!